take it to the hoOp, Magic JohnSon

By Quincy Troupe
Illustrated by Shane W. Evans

JUMP AT THE SUN
Hyperion Books for Children
New York

take it
to the

hoop,

"magic" johnson,

take the ball dazzling down the open lane

herk & jerk & raise your

six-foot, nine-inch frame

into air **sweating** screams
of your **neon** name

"Windex" Johnson

"magic" johnson, nicknamed "Windex"

Mary-Marie Askins

Benjamen Bajeedah

Christophe Bushemi

Betty Evans

JungSung Kim

Clarence Lynn

Lee Michael

Warren Vance

Paulette Walter

way back in high school
'cause you wiped glass backboards so clean,
where you first juked & shook,
wiled your way to glory

a *new-style* fusion of Shake 'n Bake
energy, using everything possible,
you created your own space to fly through—

any moment now
we expect your wings to spread
feathers for that spooky takeoff
 of yours

then, **shake & glide & ride** up in space
till you hammer home a clothes–lining deuce off glass
now,
come back down with a **reverse hoodoo** gem
off the spin & stick in **sweet,** popping
nets clean from **twenty** feet, right side

so put the **ball** on the floor again, "**magic**"

s l i d e the dribble behind your back,

ease it deftly between your bony stork
      legs, head **bobbing** everwhichaway

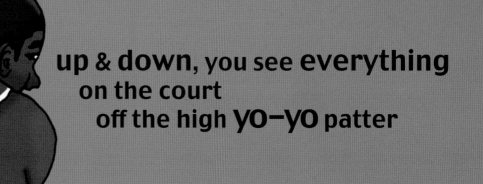

up & down, you see **everything**
  on the court
    off the high **yo-yo** patter

stop & **go** dribble
    you thread a needle–rope pass sweet home

now, lead the fastbreak,
hit **worthy** on the fly

now, **blindside** a pinpoint
behind-the-back pass
for two more off the fake,
looking the other way,
you raise off-balance into
electric space
sweating chants of your
name

turn, 180 degrees off the
move, your legs scissoring
space
like a swimmer's
yo-yoing motion in
deep water
stretching out now
toward free flight
you double-pump
through human trees
hang in place

slip the ball into
your **left** hand

then deal it like a las vegas card dealer off squared glass into nets, living up to your singular **nickname**

so "bad" you cartwheel the crowd
toward frenzy, wearing now your
electric smile, neon as your name

in victory, we suddenly sense your
glorious uplift, your urgent need to be
champion
& so we cheer with you,
rejoice with you for this
quicksilver, **quicksilver**,
quicksilver moment of fame

so put
the **ball**
on the
floor again,
"magic"

**juke & dazzle,
Shake 'n Bake
down the lane**

take the sucker to the hoop,
"magic" johnson,

recreate

reverse

hoodoo

gems

off the spin

deal alley-oop **dunkathon**
magician passes
now, **double-pump,**
scissor, vamp through space

hang in place

& put it all up in the sucker's face, "magic" johnson,

& deal the roundball like the juju man that you am like the sho-nuff shaman that you am, "magic,"

like the sho-nuff spaceman you am

For my grandchildren, Amina Grace, André-El, Courtney, Crystal,
Jonathan, Lillian, and Samuel, and my youngest son, Porter
—Q.T.

Thank you, GOD.
Dedicated to all of my aunts and uncles
for helpin' me "Take it to the hoop!"
—S.W.E.

the end.

Printed in Hong Kong
First edition
1 3 5 7 9 10 8 6 4 2

This book is set in Charcoal.
Library of Congress Cataloging-in-Publication Data
Troupe, Quincy.
Take it to the hoop, Magic Johnson/ Quincy Troupe ; illustrated by Shane Evans.-1st ed.
p. cm.
Summary: A poetic celebration of Magic Johnson and his quicksilver moments of
triumph on the basketball court.
ISBN 0-7868-0510-2 (trade) - ISBN 0-7868-2446-8 (library)
1. Johnson, Earvin, 1959-Juvenile poetry. 2. Basketball players-Juvenile poetry.
3. Afro-Americans-Juvenile poetry. 4. Basketball-Juvenile poetry. 5. Children's poetry,
American. [1. Johnson, Earvin, 1959-Poetry. 2. Basketball-Poetry. 3.
Afro-Americans-Poetry. 4. American poetry.] I. Evans, Shane, ill. II. Title.

PS3570.R63 T35 2000
811'.54-dc21
00-020407

Visit www.jumpatthesun.com

I'm the Big One Now!

Poems about Growing Up

Marilyn Singer

Illustrated by **Jana Christy**

WORDSONG

Honesdale, Pennsylvania

Contents

A THOUSAND THINGS MORE

A picture of me

when I was just three,

    dancing across the floor.

Still got the same nose,

    still strike the same pose,

       but I now know a thousand things more.

TAKING THE BUS

Not big enough
    to drive a car
    (or my bike real far),
    to grow a beard
    (plus I'd look weird),

    to stay up late
    (like, way past eight),
    to own a phone . . .
But plenty big
    to take a bus
    without a fuss
    and go to school
    ALONE!

TRYING TO RIDE, PART 1

It's the biggest of really big deals:

   riding my bike on two wheels.

It's red and it's just the right size.

   I can't wait to feel how it flies.

Now here I am in the school yard,

   but why is this coasting so hard?

And how do I pedal *and* steer?

   I hope this won't take me all year . . .

FIRST GOOD SNAP,
A Poem for

Like the sound of the moon . . .

Like a drum before it's struck . . .

I'm saying it was silent:

When I snapped, no one heard it.

Suddenly, aha!

My fingers now can do it.

To think I couldn't snap

Not so long . . .

ago.

FIRST GOOD WHISTLE:
Two Voices

Like a leaky old balloon . . .

Like a really tired duck . . .

I'm saying it was lame:

When I whistled, no one came.

All at once, oh!

My lips know how to blow.

To think I couldn't whistle

Oh, so long . . .

9

IN THE THEATRE

Everyone says I'm noisy
    like a circus, like a riot.
But here, in the theatre, I *want* to be quiet,
    sitting in my seat, velvety, deep.
Lights down! Curtain up!
    On stage, a princess is asleep.
I will not let out one peep.

AT THE BALLPARK

Everyone says I'm quiet,
     like the grass, like the sky.
But here, in the ballpark,
     when I'm part of the crowd,
I say to myself, *I'm allowed to be LOUD!*
So when the rookie batter swings and scores,
     this rookie fan jumps up and ROARS!

FIRST TIME LEFT, FIRST TIME RIGHT

Left.

This one is left.

I think that's right.

I mean, it's left.

The one that's left

    I'm sure is right.

Whoa, it's like somebody turned on a light!

I'm so bright and excited.

I've left and I've righted

    my hands. Now it's time for my feet.

Wait—that's not it . . .

Wait . . . I've got it!

Sweet!

COUNTING MONEY

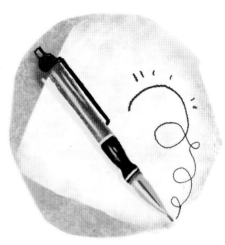

Ten pennies, two nickels, one little dime—
    I'm buying a ball for the very first time.
Ten nickels, five dimes, and, look, here's a quarter—
    I'm turning into a good money sorter!
I can count all the change that makes up a dollar.
    I can purchase a pen, buy my poodle a collar!
I can get Mom a hammer. I can buy Dad a grater.
    (Then maybe he'll make us a pizza pie later.)
I can spend it or save it in my piggy bank
    for a guitar for Grandma, a giant fish tank,
a trip to the Rockies that someday I'll climb,
    thanks to those pennies, those nickels, that dime.

COOKING FOR MOM

This Saturday morning in January,
      the sky is as gray as my woolly hat.
Mom is sniffling, sneezing,
      staring out her bedroom window with a sigh.
I decide to give her July
      for breakfast,
my first cooking-alone try
      (with Dad standing by):
Eggs, sunny-side up
      on a bright blue plate;
Butter, a golden pat perched
      on a blanket of toast;
Slices of banana
      sailing in a fruity boat;
A cup of tea
      with a lemon-circle float.
Dad makes a tissue paper carnation,
      lays it on a tray.
We know it's worthwhile
      when Mom says, "Just my style,"
and gives us her summer-vacation smile.

TRYING TO RIDE, Part 2

My brother rode his bike at six,
  and now he can do fancy tricks,
while I wobble, shimmy, and shake,
  then flop to the ground when I brake.
Mom says I *will* learn the technique—
  I'm better than I was last week.
And Dad says that Mom's never wrong.
  And *I* say it's taking too long!

BIG KIDS DO CRY

It hurt with a hurt
      that I couldn't ignore,
Like a shot burning hot
      I had not felt before.
And I thought, *I can't cry.*
      I'm not three—I'm not four.
Till Dad said, "Go ahead."
      Then I let my tears pour.
Now, I wouldn't cry
      for a toy in a store.
Or after a game
      'cause I got a low score.
Or out in the yard
      if my favorite pants tore.
But things like beestings?
      Well, that's what crying's for!

MY OWN SEAT ON THE PLANE

Last time—I hardly remember—
I was on Mama's lap.
And all I did was nap.
But today, in my very own seat,
I am trying not to wiggle,
    not to giggle
too much while we taxi to the runway—
    first a glide, then a rev and a roar
        as we jutter, shudder,
        lift off, climb.
I touch the new pin on my shirt—
    a small pair of wings—
And this time, leaning into my own seat,
    something in me sings.

FIRST VISIT TO THE OCEAN

Seeing it on TV

doesn't tell you how big the ocean is,

    or how salty it tastes

when a wave sprays your face,

    how it can erase

        footprints, messages, castles with moats,

    how it welcomes gulls and clams and all kinds of boats,

doesn't show how you leave the city so far behind

    and arrive in a country so new

you imagine you're a dolphin

    in that wide, wide world of blue.

FIRST BIG-KID PARTY

We drive to the party.
We walk to the door.
"Have fun!" says my mom.
"I'll be back at four."

I take a big gulp
as I wave good-bye.
I feel kind of bold,
I feel kind of shy.

I know only some
of the kids in the room.
I stand in a corner
as still as a broom.

Then Jake (it's his birthday)
says, "Here's your disguise.
Tom is your partner.
We're all private eyes."

We're off on a case.
We follow the clues.
We're working together—
so how can we lose?

We figure it out!
We let out a hoot.
We find in the doghouse
a big bag of loot!

There's mystery cake
and I'm laughing with Tom.
We're trading moustaches,
when here comes my mom.

I got to be clever.
I made a new friend.
I'm sorry this party
has come to an end.

But next week is Tom's.
And I am invited!
I won't be a broom.
'Cause I'll be too excited!

Happy Birthday!

Party!

Max

21

HOW DELICIOUS!

I am sniffing the ink and smoothing the paper,
    remembering when I bit covers and licked pages,
    when I thought words were something
        to eat.
But today,
   today instead,
   I READ.
And I didn't use my teeth or tongue,
    like some hungry beast
to gobble that scrumptious alphabet feast.

BIG-KID TEETH

My big-kid teeth
are underneath
these baby ones
which feel unsteady—
wiggly, wobbly getting ready
to fall out.
Two are so loose
they could land in my juice!
I pretend I'm a shark with row after row—
such a big snout of them
they never run out of them.
But Mom says, "Nope, just one more set.
Those big-kid teeth are all you get."
I tell her that it's so unfair.
Kids, like sharks, can use a spare!

CANNONBALL

Yesterday I stood and stared
  at the blue bottom
  of this big pool.
Yesterday, and the day before,
  and the day before that.

But today,
   today,
I hold my breath.
I do not freeze.
I jump up high
  and grab my knees.
Like a coconut, I drop
  with a smashing splash,
touch my toes to that blue bottom,
  and, in a flash, up I pop.
My heart's thump-thumping—
I love this jumping,
  rising, falling,
  this cannonballing.
I'll do it forever—

till someone makes me stop.

FIRST BALLET RECITAL,
A Poem for

I have to remember to point my toe

and bend my knees in a plié,

To stand straight like I'm at the barre.

If I mess up, I cannot stop.

The music is starting. I'm going on now.

I'm taking the stage. It's my turn to dance!

FIRST PIANO RECITAL:
Two Voices

I have to remember where my hands go.

I have to know which notes to play

for "Twinkle, Twinkle, Little Star."

I can't start over from the top.
I must not forget to begin with a bow.

Here are the keys. Here is my chance!

TRYING TO RIDE,
Part 3

Yippee and yahoo and yay!
    I no longer teeter or sway.
I'm pedaling in a straight line.
    I'm braking at every stop sign.
And look, I can turn left or right.
    Can I zip down a hill? Well, not quite.
But I know I'll be doing that soon—
    by Sunday afternoon!

HOLDING MY NEW BROTHER FOR THE FIRST TIME

Still as the stone frog
      in the yard, by the daisies,
I sit, trying to breathe the way he breathes,
      so deep and slow.
But my mind is hopping like a real frog,
      in woods, by the pond:
I'm first. I'm not the only.
I'm young. But I'm the older.
Wow.
I'm the big one now.

To Yonatan, Yuval, and Ethan Jeremiah, who will be big ones one day soon!
—MS

For Harry and Hugo
—JC

WordSong
An Imprint of Highlights
815 Church Street
Honesdale, Pennsylvania 18431
wordsongpoetry.com
Printed in China

ISBN: 978-1-62979-169-2
Library of Congress Control Number: 2018903175

First edition
10 9 8 7 6 5 4 3 2 1

The text of this book is set in Rotis Sans Serif Light.
The drawings are digital.